FLOWERS
FOR ALL SEASONS
FALL

Also by Jane Packer

Celebrating with Flowers
Flowers for All Seasons: Spring
Flowers for All Seasons: Summer
Flowers for All Seasons: Winter

FLOWERS
FOR ALL SEASONS
FALL

Text by Jane Packer and Elizabeth Wilhide

Fawcett Columbine · New York

A Fawcett Columbine Book
Published by Ballantine Books

Text Copyright © 1989 by Pavilion Books Limited
Concept Copyright © 1989 by Jane Packer
Photographs Copyright © 1989 by Di Lewis
Palette illustrations © 1989 by Linda Smith
Line illustrations © 1989 by Gill Elsbury

Originally published in Great Britain as *Flowers for All Seasons: Autumn*
in 1989 by Pavilion Books Limited.

Library of Congress Cataloguing-in-Publication Data

Packer, Jane
    Flowers for all seasons: fall/text by Jane Packer and Elizabeth
Wilhide—1st American ed.
        p. cm.
    "A Fawcett Columbine book"—T.p. verso.
    Includes index.
    ISBN 0-449-90413-X
    1. Flower arrangement. 2. Flowers. 3. Autumn. I. Wilhide,
Elizabeth. II. Title III. Title: Fall.
SB449.P222   1989
745.92—dc20
                                                            88-92868
                                                                CIP
Printed and bound in Spain by Cayfosa Industria Grafica.

First American Edition: September 1989

10 9 8 7 6 5 4 3 2 1

Contents

Introduction 6

Fall Flowers and Foliage 8

The Fall Palette 12

A Style for Fall 22

Fall Weddings 54

Special Occasions 74

Basic Techniques 100

Index 110

Acknowledgements 111

Introduction

Leaves turning on the trees, an invigorating nip in the air and branches laden with clusters of bright berries mean that fall has arrived. Like spring, fall is a season of change. In the garden, flowers become scarce and leaves begin to drop. The mood is wistful and rather melancholy.

But fall is a time of abundance as well as a time of decline. Fruits ripen ready for harvest, an event celebrated around the world in traditional festivals of thanksgiving. Although fall imposes certain limitations in terms of flower variety, as always it is far more effective and satisfying to express the mood of the season in your arrangements than to rely solely on commercially cultivated flowers or imported varieties. At this time of year, I find myself creating displays which are heavier and more solid in structure, which somehow seem to suggest a fall instinct for gathering and storing. Colours are typically rich and glowing – russets, reds, golds and oranges – entirely appropriate for creating a sense of warmth as the days grow cooler.

Above all, fall is a time when you can extend the possibilities by trying out exciting and imaginative combinations of fruit, vegetables, foliage and dried flowers – a natural cornucopia perfectly in keeping with the season. Fall leaves are so colourful that they more than make up for a scarcity of flowers; pine cones, rosehips, shiny chestnuts lend a depth of texture; clusters of berries, ripe gourds or a bowl of apples can express the mood of abundance. Dried flowers are an evocative reminder of the glories of summer.

The beauty of fall lies in its imperfection. Flowers may be a little windswept; leaves are burnt by frost; branches are almost bare. But there is something particularly romantic about arrangements which try to capture this rather poignant atmosphere and reflect what is really happening outdoors.

JANE PACKER

Fall Flowers
and Foliage

Fall abundance does not extend to flower colour or variety. In the garden, most of the summer flowers have died down, leaving isolated clumps of vivid colour. The fall palette is generally in the warm spectrum of gold through russet to red. Light pinks and other pastels have all but disappeared.

In terms of foliage, summer lushness has given way to branches which are becoming bare; displaying, nevertheless, a certain stark beauty of their own. Some leaves, notably maple, turn spectacular shades of red, gold and yellow, rivalling any flower; stems laden with bunches of berries are another useful supplement from the garden. One important word of warning: many fall berries are poisonous. Some can cause an unpleasant bout of sickness; others are so lethal that only two or three could kill a child. If, like me, you find yourself attracted to a vivid spray of berries, please check in a reliable plant-finder that you are not bringing an unnecessary risk into the home. Unfortunately, the brighter berries are often the more dangerous ones.

Inevitably, the garden cannot be the only source of material in the fall months. In addition to florist's flowers, either seasonal or imported, it is worth investigating and exploiting the potential of dried varieties. Many summer flowers are easy to dry, providing a welcome reminder of warmer days as well as extending the possibilities for arrangements.

SELECTING FLOWERS
Buying in bud is advisable for most flowers: it is better to select flowers which are still in bud to make the most of their short life. Avoid tight green buds which may never open and opt for those which are showing a little colour.

Always check any flowers wrapped in plastic lining for

Right: A grey-green arrangement of foliage tones with the monochrome setting. The display includes eucalyptus and eucalyptus buds, sloe, rhododendron and variegated ivy (canariensis).

8

signs of botrytis or mildew. Flowers which have been kept wrapped for several days will sweat because of the lack of ventilation and stems and foliage will begin to rot. This can be a particular problem in the fall if the flowers have been packed while they were wet.

In rainy weather, check that the flowers have not been left standing for hours outdoors. Chrysanthemums suffer quickly, becoming battered and losing their petals.

SOURCES

A good florist is the best source for healthy fresh flowers and will stock a wider range of colours and varieties than the average market stall or corner shop. Shops which only carry flowers as a sideline – petrol stations, for example – may be less reliable. A lack of trained staff and a slower turnover of stock can lead to flowers being displayed when they are past their best.

Florists' flowers used to be synonymous with highly cultivated hothouse blooms, to the extent that when "garden" flowers became more commonly available in shops, people showed a certain reluctance to buy them. With fashion now swinging away from the formal and exotic in favour of natural effects, there is less of a distinction between what you can see growing in a garden and what is on sale in a flower shop. The biggest difference is that many flowers appear much earlier in the flower shops than they do in the garden, by virtue of the flowers being commercially cultivated or flown in from warmer areas. And, of course, it is useful to remember that florists can supply many types of flower virtually all year round, which act as a useful supplement to a seasonal range.

Planning and planting a garden to create a source of cut flowers for the home is a subject in itself. But unless beds and borders are overflowing with blooms, most people have to compromise between having colour indoors or out. In the fall, there are likely to be so few flowers growing in the garden that picking them for indoors arrangements is not a practical proposition. Instead, concentrate on collecting chestnuts, leaves, branches and interesting vines. Even when devoid of

Right: A cheerful collection of jugs in motley colours, sizes and shapes are used to display a mixture of fall flowers in the warm shades of yellow through to bronze. Varieties include rosehips, and miniature chrysanthemums.

foliage, honeysuckle, for example, can be intriguingly knotted and twisted.

Hedgerows, verges and neglected patches of land can also provide plentiful sources of foliage and of trailing stems such as ivy. Remember, however, that wild flowers should never be picked. Areas of true woodland, wild meadows and hedgerows are fast declining, with the loss of many species and it is important to leave the flowers and plants untouched to aid their conservation.

The Fall Palette

ACHILLEA (Yarrow; *Achillea* sp.)
Availability July–October; cut or garden
Price Cheap, or free from garden
Colour range White, yellow, pink, purple
Life span Long-lasting
Mass of florets at the end of a long stem. Remove foliage below the water line. Achillea is a good filler and easy to dry. Sharp mustard yellow variety is very useful in combinations; colour remains vivid even when the flower is dried.

ALSTROEMERIA (Peruvian lily; *Alstroemeria* hybrid)
Availability Year-round; cut
Price Medium
Colour range White, yellow, pink, orange, red, purple
Life span Very long-lasting
There is an average of four flowers and buds on each long stem, with frail, delicate foliage. This lily-like flower is less expensive and much more resilient than it looks. Buds will continue to open. Use on its own or in mixed arrangements. Excellent wedding flower.

AMARANTHUS (*Amaranthus* sp.)
Availability September–November; cut
Price Medium
Colour range Green, red
Life span Long-lasting
Short stem, brush-like upright flower. Provides textural interest rather than beauty. Easy to dry. Not really suitable for displaying on its own.

AMARYLLIS (*Hippeastrum* hybrids)
Availability September–March; cut or potted
Price Expensive
Colour range White, pink, peach, red
Life span Very long-lasting
Trumpet flowers at the end of a long tubular, foliage-free stem. Buy in tight bud for a long life. Looks stark and modern used on its own; or cut flower heads low into a bowl. Dramatic and resilient flower for weddings.

ANEMONE (*Anemone coronaria*)
Availability September–May; cut
Price Cheap to medium (long-stemmed)
Colour range White, pink, purple, deep red, blue
Life span Long-lasting
Velvety petals surrounding a black centre. Cheap short-stemmed variety are best massed in jugs for a rich, cottagey look; intense colour can suggest an Eastern look. Long-stemmed or single colour bunches are more sophisticated. Suits wedding bouquets; "The Bride", a white anemone, has a Victorian appeal.

ASTER (Michaelmas daisy; *Aster novia-belgii*)
Availability October–November; cut
Price Cheap
Colour range White, pink, orange, purple
Life span Long-lasting
Cottage garden appeal; easy to grow. Choose simple, unpretentious containers and mass the flowers or combine in country-style mixtures.

BANKSIA
Availability July–November; cut
Price Expensive
Colour range Golden or pinkish
Life span Very long-lasting
Unusual-looking thistle grown in hot climates. Provides textural interest and strong form; not for soft or flowing displays. Dries easily.

BOX (*Buxus sempervirens*)
Availability Year-round; cut or garden
Price Cheap or free from garden
Colour range Dark green or variegated foliage
Life span Very long-lasting
Invaluable year-round foliage. Small leaves massed on long branches; will grow long or can be clipped. Use to make artificial topiary or as a strong support in large arrangements (branches are quite stiff). Leaves do not drop; pungent smell.

BRODIAEA
Availability Year-round; cut
Price Medium
Colour range Blue or white
Life span Long-lasting
A cluster of bell-type flowers on top of a thin, foliage-free stem. An important source of blue in the autumn months. Display dainty flowers in a bud vase, or combine in mixtures; expensive to mass on its own.

CARNATION (*Dianthus* sp.)
Availability Year-round; cut
Price Cheap
Colour range White, pink, red, purple; also striated, speckled or edged
Life span Very long-lasting
Popular and well-known flower, commonly used as buttonholes for weddings or functions, or in mixed formal arrangements. Buy half-open, without any white stamens showing in the centre. The centre of the flower should feel hard and compact when pressed. Slight perfume.

CELOSIA (*Celosia argentea* hybrids)
Availability July–October; cut
Price Expensive
Colour range Gold, pink, purple, red
Life span Long-lasting
Resembles crushed velvet; interesting texture. Can be used as a filler or displayed on its own with stems left long for a stark, dramatic focal point. Dries very easily.

CHRYSANTHEMUM (*Chrysanthemum* hybrids)
Availability Year-round; cut, potted or garden
Price Cheap
Colour range White, pink, red, bronze, yellow, purple
Life span Very long-lasting
Common in late summer to early-fall in the garden. There are many different varieties, including single blooms and sprays. Size can range from tiny heads ½in (1.5cm) in diameter to heads up to 8in (20cm) in diameter.

The single, daisy-like chrysanthemum, available in sprays or individual blooms, has a green centre and is useful for creating a country look in arrangements or for wedding bouquets. Wide colour range, including pastels. Buds should not be discarded – they can add a dainty look to a posy or small arrangement.

The double chrysanthemum, also available in sprays or single blooms, has petals which completely cover the centre. This variety is particularly associated with the garden and is normally cheaper.

Other common varieties include the spider chrysanthemum, with its spiky petals and Oriental appearance, and the ball or pom pom, with its dense round head. All have a strong, herbal smell and blooms can shatter easily if knocked.

COTONEASTER (*Cotoneaster horizontalis*)
Availability Year-round; berries from September to January from garden
Price Free from garden
Colour range Dark green leaves, red berries
Life span Very long-lasting
Clusters of bright red berries and small dark leaves on stiff thorny branches. A good source of colour and texture when flowers are scarce. Can be mixed with other autumn foliage. Hammer the stems to aid uptake of water.

CRAB APPLE (*Malus* sp.)
Availability August–October; cut from garden
Price Free from garden
Colour range Green to yellow foliage, with green, yellow, red or purple fruit
Life span Long-lasting
Cut branches arc gently to create flowing lines. Alternatively, use in a vase on its own for a stunning focal point. Woody stems should be hammered to aid uptake of water.

CYNARA (*Cynara scolymus*)
Availability July–October; cut
Price Medium
Colour range Purple
Life span Very long-lasting
Heads are dramatic looking and very large, giving the appearance of a Scottish thistle. Use in large arrangements or to create a "landscape" effect. Can be very striking in a vase on its own, with the stems left long. Easy to dry.

DAHLIA (*Dahlia* hybrids)
Availability July–September; cut
Price Cheap
Colour range White, pink, red, purple, yellow, bronze, orange; also speckled
Life span Short life
Huge variety of size, colour and flower type; an old-fashioned garden flower with many devotees. Vivid, almost garish colours can be fun. Use in small arrangements, or in vases on its own. The fleshy stems begin to decay very quickly, so change the water daily to avoid strong rotting smell.

ECHINOPS (Globe-thistle; *Echinops ritro*)
Availability September–November; cut
Price Cheap
Colour range Blue or white
Life span Very long-lasting
A globe thistle, with silvery foliage and a very stiff stem. Cluster heads for colour and textural impact – more of a dramatic than a beautiful flower. Dries very easily.

ELAEAGNUS (*Elaeagnus* sp.)
Availability Year-round; cut
Price Medium, or free from garden
Colour range Silvery green or yellow variegated foliage
Life span Long-lasting
Glossy leaf with a grey-white, papery underside. Excellent foliage for arrangements and wedding work. Leaf is very robust and since both sides are interesting, the leaf can be wired from the top or the bottom.

ERYNGIUM (*Eryngium* sp.)
Availability May–November; cut
Price Medium
Colour range Dark blue
Life span Very long-lasting
Small thistle surrounded by a large collar of silvery fronds. Can look very modern on its own, or use clustered in fall arrangements.

EUPHORBIA (*Spurgens Euphorbia fulgens*)
Availability October–March; cut
Price Expensive
Colour range White, cream, apricot, orange, red
Life span Long-lasting
A long arced stem, one-third covered in clusters of small flowers and foliage; resembles orange blossom. Use in tall vases or in large arrangements to show off soft, flowing line. Good for wedding work. Stems exude a sap which can cause skin irritation; seal cut stems by holding in a flame for two seconds.

FREESIA (*Freesia* hybrids)
Availability Year-round; cut
Price Medium
Colour range White, cream, yellow, orange, red, mauve
Life span Long-lasting
Extremely popular flower, with a pervasive, fruity scent. Commercial varieties are available with longer stems and in single colour bunches, and are more expensive. Use in clear containers to emphasize fine stems. Lasts well wired in wedding bouquets although it has a delicate appearance. Avoid placing near food because of strong scent.

GERBERA (Transvaal daisy; *Gerbera jamesonii*)
Availability Year-round; cut or potted
Price Medium
Colour range White, pink, red, apricot, yellow, orange
Life span Long-lasting
Single variety resembles a daisy; also a fuller, double variety. Long, foliage-free stem; flower has a simple, childlike appearance. If stems are weak, support them by wrapping in paper and place in water. Once water has been taken up, the stems will strengthen and straighten.

GLADIOLUS (Sword lily; *Gladiolus* hybrids)
Availability July–November; cut
Price Medium
Colour range White, pink, orange, red, cream, apricot, purple
Life span Long-lasting
Strong, elegant stem, with clusters of lily-like flowers. Excellent used on its own in vases; florets can be wired individually for wedding work. Avoid positioning in stark, stiff lines.

HEATHER (*Erica* sp.)
Availability September–November (flowering); cut or potted
Price Medium
Colour range White to deep pink, purple
Life span Long-lasting
Stiff, with plumes of florets. Good filler for solid-looking arrangements; can also be effective in a basket on its own. White heather is a symbol of good luck and is popular for weddings. Easy to dry.

HEBE (*Hebe* sp.)
Availability September–November; cut or potted
Price Medium
Colour range Dark or variegated leaves; white or purple flower
Life span Long-lasting
Small dark or variegated fleshy leaves, with small flower at tip of stem. Use as a foliage. Branches are stiff. The tiny flower makes a useful colour accent.

HELICHRYSUM (Straw flower; *Helichrysum bracteatum*)
Availability August–October; cut or garden
Price Cheap
Colour range White, yellow, orange, purple, pink, red
Life span Long-lasting
Very old-fashioned flower, with a velvety centre and papery petals. Easy to dry and more commonly used dried than fresh.

HYDRANGEA (*Hydrangea* sp.)
Availability April–November; cut or garden
Price Medium; free from garden
Colour range White, pink, green, blue, lilac, red
Life span Long-lasting
One of the most common garden shrubs. Can be cut and used low as a basis for an arrangement or in a low vase to display heads. Individual bracts can also be wired for wedding work. Easy to dry. Paler colours turn to richer shades in the fall. Lace cap variety has a hazy appearance.

IVY (*Hedera helix* "Arborescens")
Availability Year-round; (fall flowering); cut or garden
Price Cheap or free
Colour range Dark green foliage, golden flower, turning black
Life span Very long-lasting
Commonly found on wasteland or neglected areas of woodland, growing up the side of a tree or wall. Huge bracts of dark glossy green leaves; unusual flowers. Useful as a filler in the centre of arrangements. Not a trailing ivy.

LAVENDER (*Lavandula angustifolia*)
Availability July–September; cut
Price Expensive
Colour range White, lavender, purple
Life span Long-lasting
Pick or buy during the summer to dry for pot pourri or to use in dried arrangements. White dries to a dingy off-white but purples get darker. Strong characteristic perfume. Tie in wheatsheaf shape; can also be used fresh and for wedding work.

LILY (Asiatic lily, *Lilium* sp.)
Availability Year-round; cut
Price Expensive
Colour range Cream, yellow, orange, apricot, pink, red
Life span Long-lasting
Star-like lily, 3½in (9cm) in diameter. Fleshy green stem with about five buds or flowers at the top. Although expensive, flowers do last very well; perfumed. Remove pollen as it will stain clothes, carpets, etc. Wide range of uses, including wedding work, cut down in low arrangements, in vases alone.

LOVE-LIES-BLEEDING (*Amaranthus caudatus* hybrids)
Availability September–October; cut
Price Medium
Colour range Green or red tassels
Life span Long-lasting
Striking flower; trailing red tassels resemble crushed velvet. Gives movement and shape to large pedestal arrangements. Trails create flowing line. Easy to dry.

MAPLE (*Acer* sp.)
Availability September–October for colour
Price Medium or free from garden
Colour range Greens, golds, reds, orange
Life span Long-lasting
Available as cut branches. Large well-shaped leaves which turn a range of vivid fall colours. Use in a vase on its own or combine in a large arrangement. Requires only a few additional complementary flowers because colours are so strong. Leaves can be glycerined to preserve them.

OAK (*Quercus* sp.)
Availability September–October for colour
Price Medium, or free from garden
Colour range Dull gold, brown
Life span Long-lasting
Duller, warmer colour than maple leaf, but similar use. Acorns also add textural interest; leaves can be glycerined.

POPPY (*Papaver* sp.)
Availability October–April; cut
Price Medium
Colour range White, pink, apricot, orange, yellow
Life span Short life
These commercially cultivated varieties are smaller than the common red poppy. Beautiful pastel shades; papery petals on slender stems; delicate, drooping neck. Seal stems by holding in a flame for 2–3 seconds. Buy in bud to prolong life. Use simply.

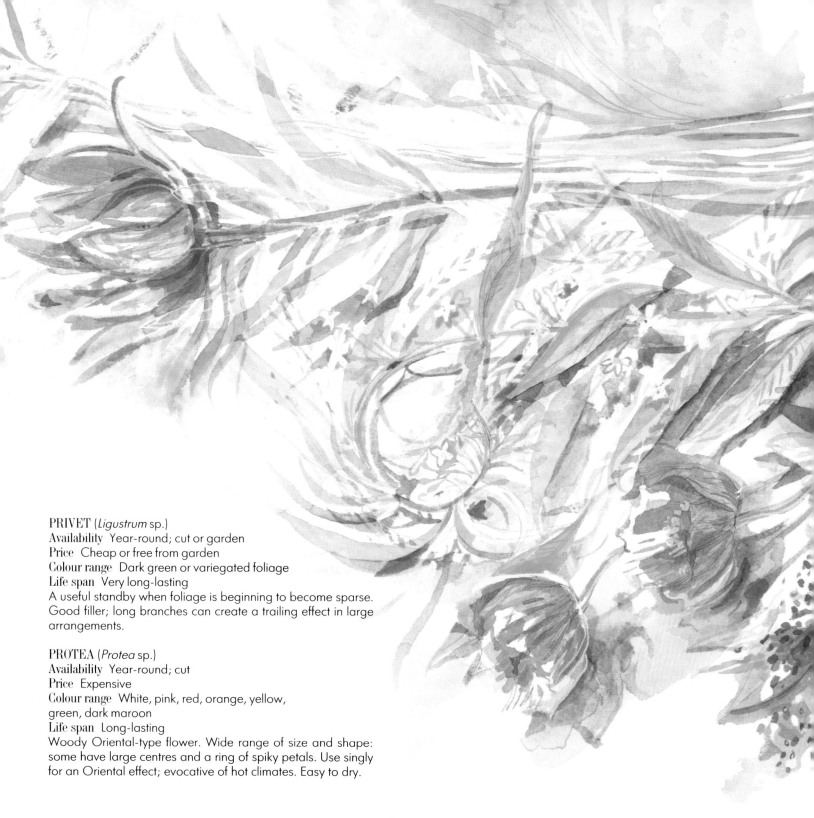

PRIVET (*Ligustrum* sp.)
Availability Year-round; cut or garden
Price Cheap or free from garden
Colour range Dark green or variegated foliage
Life span Very long-lasting
A useful standby when foliage is beginning to become sparse.
Good filler; long branches can create a trailing effect in large
arrangements.

PROTEA (*Protea* sp.)
Availability Year-round; cut
Price Expensive
Colour range White, pink, red, orange, yellow,
green, dark maroon
Life span Long-lasting
Woody Oriental-type flower. Wide range of size and shape:
some have large centres and a ring of spiky petals. Use singly
for an Oriental effect; evocative of hot climates. Easy to dry.

RANUNCULUS (*Ranunculus asiaticus* hybrids)
Availability October–March; cut (commercially cultivated)
Price Expensive
Colour range White, pink, orange, red
Life span Long-lasting
Dense head of petals, curved stems. Buy when head is fairly compact; will continue to open. Heads often droop: arrange to emphasize the natural line rather than attempt to position straight. Excellent wedding flower; can be dried.

ROSE (*Rosa* sp.)
Availability Year-round; cut
Price Medium to expensive
Colour range White, pink, red, cream, yellow, apricot, orange, lavender
Life span Long-lasting
Roses commercially available in the fall have straight upright stems and tend to look rather formal. By using flowers which are fully open and combining colours you can create more of a natural impression. Wrap flowers in paper and place in deep water for two hours to make sure heads do not drop.

SKIMMIA (*Skimmia japonica*)
Availability September–November (flowering); cut and potted
Price Expensive
Colour range White or red flower; red berries; gold or green foliage
Life span Very long-lasting
Use as foliage. Stiff branches, with glossy, waxy leaves. Berries make useful colour accent. Good filler; can be wired for wedding work.

STATICE (Everlasting; *Limonium sinuatum*)
Availability September–November; cut
Price Cheap
Colour range White, yellow, pink, lavender, purple
Life span Very long-lasting
Clusters of small flowers available in large bunches; "sea lavender" variety has white plumes. Dries easily and is very common in dried arrangements.

VIBURNUM (*Viburnum tinus*)
Availability September–January flowering; cut
Price Medium
Colour range Pinky white flower; green foliage
Life span Very long-lasting
Knotty branches with short clusters of dark green leaves, flowers and black berries. Common garden shrub in the South and West. Excellent for small arrangements or as a filler for a pedestal display. Good for wedding work.

VIRGINIA CREEPER (*Parthenocissus quinquefolia*)
Availability September–October for colour; garden
Price Free from garden
Colour range Red
Life span Short life
Trails of bright red leaves look stunning in large arrangements, laid along a table or even in wedding bouquets. Leaves begin to drop once they have turned red, so life span is very short.

WHEAT (*Triticum* sp.)
Availability May (in the South); August–October(elsewhere); cut
Price Cheap
Colour range Green to golden yellow
Life span Long-lasting
Tasselled grain, with grass-like foliage. Obvious connotation with the fall and harvest time. Use in bunches, not scattered individually. Can be bunched and tied wheatsheaf-shape, in or out of water. Evocative door decoration. Easy to dry and preserve.

YEAR ROUND FLOWERS
Although some of the following flowers and foliage are associated with a particular season, they are generally available year-round from florists and flower stalls, and make a useful supplement to the typical seasonal range.
*indicates description in text.

*ALSTROEMERIA	GYPSOPHILA
*BOX	IRIS
*CARNATION	*IVY
*CHRYSANTHEMUM	LAUREL
CUPRESSUS	*LILY
EUCALYPTUS	MOSS
*FREESIA	ORCHID
*GLADIOLUS	*ROSE

A Style for Fall

As the days grow cooler and the nights draw in, it always seems appropriate to create arrangements which suggest a sense of warmth and solidity. Rich colour mixtures of yellow, gold, orange and red are particularly cheerful and welcoming. Displays can be heavier and more substantial-looking than at other times of the year, anchored both visually and practically by sturdy containers such as earthenware pots and robust baskets.

There is a strong tradition for combining fruit, vegetable and flowers in harvest-festival style arrangements — a strategy which obviously extends the creative scope and looks almost more natural during the fall than at any other time of the year. The additional colour supplied by these elements is a bonus when the range of flowers is limited; different textures give depth and interest. The use of dried flowers is another way of supplementing the fall palette of fresh flowers and foliage, and represents one particular aspect of floral design which has been expanded and invigorated by new ideas and techniques over the last ten years.

Above left: Fall is a time associated with harvest. Here dried wheat sheaves strike a suitably rustic note. Several pots of white heather are massed in the container on the left.

Right: Bronze chrysanthemum plants emphasize the warm terracotta tones of this brick fireplace.

COLOUR

Colour is an important means of conveying the fall mood. Silvery foliages, cool blue or shimmering white flowers, for example, display a natural freshness which is perfectly suited to the warmer spring and summer weather. In the fall, however, when light levels are lower, these pale shades can look washed-out and chilly. The vivid and welcoming tints of deep yellow, gold, orange, bronze, red and burgundy are much more effective at counteracting the natural gloom. Rich combinations of these shades can also help to suggest a sense of abundance at a time when the range of flower varieties are becoming rather limited.

Left: An all-white arrangement of arum lilies, casablanca lilies, white euphorbia and the silvery foliage of eucalyptus makes a striking focal point in front of a gilded mirror.

Seasonal colour associations should be borne in mind when selecting florist's flowers to supplement what is available from the garden. The same flower, produced year round commercially, can look very different depending on how it is used in a colour combination. "Rosita" for example, a small dusty pink lily, will be supremely summery in a soft pastel mixture of pink and cream roses. The same variety, however, looks distinctly richer and warmer combined with deep reds and russets, and with polished chestnuts and rosy pink pomegranates. Similarly, yellow gerbera looks bright and breezy arranged with white daisies; when mixed with bronze and gold chrysanthemums and wheat-sheaves, it has more of a harvest-festival appeal.

POSITION

Practically speaking, flowers should be positioned where they will not be subject to extremes of temperature and where they will also not present an obstacle or hazard. Heat sources, such as radiators, working fireplaces, hobs, ovens and warm areas such as steamy bathrooms should be avoided; some flowers also object to cold, draughty locations. Do not place large or trailing displays directly in a main thoroughfare where they may easily be upset.

The key to positioning flowers effectively is eyeline. Mantelpieces suit displays that are meant to be viewed from standing height – as you come into a room, for example. Hallways are often a good location, since flowers will be the first, welcoming sight that visitors see as they enter your home. Many fall arrangements, with their clusters of fruit, berries and vegetables are well suited to display on tabletops or sideboards. And low-level arrangements, using short flowers or flowers which have been cut down, need to be viewed from above and are best positioned on a hearth, or coffee table. Less conventionally, you can draw attention to an unusual or beautiful feature by decorating it with flowers or foliage: ivy trailing over a chairback; a posy threaded around a hatstand; a mirror garlanded with dried flowers are all eye-catching displays.

Below: Dark blackberries entwine a wrought-iron candlestick. Interesting berries and foliage are an important supplement to the fall range.

CONTAINERS

Containers can range from plastic florist's trays designed to be hidden from view to the most elegant and expensive porcelain vase. But although a good variety of different containers – in terms of size, shape and style – is essential for the flower arranger, you do not have to spend a fortune. Many effective and interesting containers can be improvised from humble everyday items, such as jugs, pots, baskets and bowls. Saucers, trays and plates make suitable reservoirs for oasis; jam jars can be tucked inside baskets waterproofed with plastic. Inexpensive glass "tanks" or cylinders in different sizes are indispensable and suit many applications – except for displays consisting of certain flowers, such as celosia, which discolour the water.

In the fall, when displays tend to consist of heavier foliages and deeper, richer colours, containers accordingly need to be more solid and substantial-looking to provide both a better visual and physical anchor. Shiny copper troughs make an excellent foil for the typical fall colours; earthenware containers of all descriptions have a forthright, unpretentious appearance.

Baskets immediately suggest a country look. There is a wide range available, from fine painted wicker to the more overtly rustic, woven from coarse grasses, vines and even dried roots and herbs. Containers for outdoor displays should never be too grand or formal. Baskets, of course, are ideal; also effective are garden containers such as terracotta pots.

The size and shape of container is just as important as its appearance or style. Tall upright containers suit long straight flowers such as gladioli with florets growing down the partial length of the stems. Wide or flared neck containers are best for displays that are intended to be full and bushy; narrow neck containers suit compact, massed or simple bunches.

TYPES OF ARRANGEMENT

I believe that flowers should be treated as a natural part of life – as an extension of one's tastes and preferences. The flowers that you display in your home should look

Right: A staggered line of protea in simple glass containers makes a powerful graphic statement in a modern room dominated by lines. Glass containers work particularly well in contemporary settings.

Above: A vivid fall mixture of rich burgundy flowers and foliage: begonia rex leaves, skimmia, roses and Virginia creeper.

like they belong, complementing the colours, mood and style of your surroundings. They should never appear to be stiff and contrived, arranged in the type of artful, formal display which often seems to suggest that an important event is about to happen.

To achieve a natural, spontaneous quality in your flower arrangements, there are a number of guidelines you can follow. If you study the pattern of growth in a garden, you will not see flowers arranged in neat triangular shapes or Hogarthian curves. Instead, species are clustered together, there are gently arcing branches and new growth tapering away at the edges. To recreate this sense of the garden, group species together, a strategy which also has the effect of helping the flowers "read" better from a distance. Place larger flowers in the centre, smaller ones towards the edges and break up the lines with trails or tendrils: stiff, blunt edges are unknown in nature.

When creating a vase arrangement, it is often best to begin at the rim of the container, so that the stems of the outer flowers provide support for the larger central flowers which will stand upright. Measure each flower against the container to estimate how much to cut from the stem, laying the flower against the container in the angle in which it will eventually be used to arrive at the correct length.

Two conventions from traditional floristry are worth considering. One is to allow one and a half times the height of flowers to container. This gives stability to the display as well as a sense of proportion, and ensures that there is enough water so that the flowers get the nourishment they need. Another useful rule is to combine flowers in odd numbers — in threes, fives and sevens — which avoids the static look that even-numbered compositions can produce.

Fall is a time when you can create designs which consist of a variety of different elements; as well as flowers, you may wish to include some of the following: fruit, berries, vegetables, branches, nuts, pine cones, grasses and driftwood. Part of the attraction of the fall is the opportunity it provides to experiment with such combinations, displays which can look rather pretentious in other seasons. But this type of mixed or combined arrangement is not as easy to create as it sounds. Without thought, a display which was intended to suggest harvest-style abundance may well end up looking like an untidy heap. To be successful, there must be some affinity between the components, in terms of colour, texture, form or theme.

Although there are no hard and fast rules for effective combinations, there are some mixtures it is better to avoid. Dried flowers do not go well with fresh ones; nor do silk flowers work with dried ones. If you are trying to create a rustic effect with moss, nuts and wheatsheaves do not spoil the arrangement by placing it in a new, bleached basket. If you are making a structured, modern display, using contorted willow twigs in a glass vase (see page 42), large single blooms would be much more in keeping with the style than, for example, spray chrysanthemums.

At the simplest level, mixtures emphasizing some common quality can be created by clustering different containers together. A vase of deep red anemones could be set beside a bowl of chestnuts, for example, or a display of bronze and russet chrysanthemums could be enhanced by a collection of small pumpkins and gourds lined up alongside.

Then there are various techniques for attaching fruit and vegetables to an arrangement, so that all the elements are integrated in one design. As fruit is usually quite heavy most of these are intended for displays created in oasis, rather than vase arrangements.

*Large, heavy varieties such as aubergine, pumpkin, cabbage and squash can be anchored with lengths of sharpened garden cane. The cane should be inserted at the angle in which you want the fruit or vegetable to be displayed. For additional securing, insert heavy florist's wire through the fruit or vegetable and wind the ends around the cane.
*Beans can be stitched together in a bunch and secured on moss or oasis with a hairpin.

*Small berries, such as blackberries, which are too little to pin, need to be placed on a flat plane specially created within the arrangement.
*Bind leeks together by wrapping a wire around the centre. Cover the wire with a leek skin, or use string or twine for a garden look.
*Attach nuts such as chestnuts with wire pushed into the shell, or use a glue gun to stick wire to the outside. Wire can be cut at an angle to make a sharpened end.

DRIED FLOWERS

Ten years or so ago, a dried flower arrangement too often meant a dusty, neglected display of luridly dyed grasses, together with a few helichrysums and statice, all looking rather more fake than dried. But like other areas of floristry, dried flower design has changed immensely; now, there is an incredible variety of dried flowers available, with new methods used to produce them.

Dried flowers will never look like fresh flowers and should never be treated as some kind of substitute for them. They are simply different; they provide different textures, different shades and different effects from the fresh flower range. In general, colours are more muted, petals are more delicate and stems are frailer – all what you would expect as the result of moisture loss.

Commercial dried flowers are produced by kiln or freeze drying, both of which are rapid processes designed to retain as much of the original colour as possible. (The quicker a flower dries, the deeper and stronger its colour.) However, there are many types of flower which are easy to dry at home, an excellent way of prolonging your enjoyment of your summer garden. Most of these have fine stems: fleshy stems are slower to dry and there is consequently more chance of the flower rotting before it has been dried successfully.

FLOWERS SUITABLE FOR HOME DRYING

Achillea	Heather (impossible to fail)
Alchemilla mollis	Helichrysum (impossible to fail)
Amaranthus	Hydrangea
Anemone	Larkspur
Celosia	Protea
Cornflower	Lavender (impossible to fail)
Cynara	Peony
Delphinium	Ranunculus
Echinops (impossible to fail)	Rose
Gypsophila	Statice (impossible to fail)

Left: Dried flowers need not look exclusively countrified, especially if intense colours are massed in simple shapes. Here a whitewashed basket holds a bold display of dried roses and lavender, arranged like a topiary hedge.

Beech and magnolia leaves both dry well, as do artichokes and wheat. The seedheads of honesty, nigella and poppy can also be dried.

DRYING METHODS

All of the flowers on the preceding list, except for hydrangeas, are best dried by hanging from the stem down in a warm place such as an airing cupboard. A greenhouse may also be a suitable location, provided the atmosphere is not steamy.

The first step is to strip the foliage from the stems, as this contains excess moisture which will only slow down the process. Then tie the flowers in small bunches to allow the air to circulate and hang them upside down. Hanging will produce straight stems – if flowers are left standing in a vase, their necks will droop. Flowers such as roses should be picked as the buds are opening but before the flower is in full bloom. Hold the partially closed head over the steam from a kettle for 20 seconds; blow hard into the centre of the flower once it has dried if you want an open flower.

Above: Dried helichrysum and alchemilla mollis echo the colours of the pottery figures. Dried arrangements require no care and can be left in place as long as you wish.

Hydrangeas dry better if they are left in a vase with 2-3 ins (5-7.5 cm) of water. Once the water has been drunk, the flower gradually dries out. If hydrangeas are hung, they tend to shrivel. Hydrangeas, as well as gypsophila, magnolia leaves, beech and alchemilla, also benefit from glycerining. Add glycerine oil to 2-3 ins (5-7.5 cm) of water in the ratio of one to three, and leave the flowers to stand. The glycerine will gradually be absorbed by the flowers and keep the petals soft.

An alternative drying method is to use silica gel. But because so many crystals are needed, this technique is really only practical for drying a small amount of flowers. You can use silica gel to dry wedding bouquets; even freesia and gardenia can be dried in this way. The whole bouquet should be buried in the crystals.

To preserve the glossy appearance of nuts such as chestnuts or to protect foodstuffs such as pasta, apply a coat of clear wood varnish.

WORKING WITH DRIED FLOWERS

Most dried flowers are fairly frail and stems may not be able to support the heads. If this is the case, stems can be replaced by wire inserted in the flower heads.

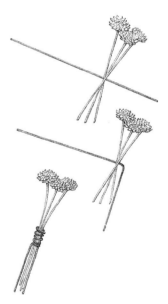

Alternatively, a mass of heads can be bound with steel wire, leaving stems intact. The technique involves making a wire stand known as a "double leg mount" which is used to hold the cluster of flowers together and insert it into moss or oasis.

Choose the gauge of wire depending on the weight of flowers. Bend one-third of the wire down and lay it onto the stems several inches above their base. Then wind the longer end several times tightly around the stems so that it finishes parallel with the first side. The two sides of the wire now facing down – the "double leg" – can then be used like a stand to hold the flowers in position.

Dried flowers are best arranged in a special type of oasis, which is harder and less crumbly than fresh flower oasis. (Dried flowers cannot be used together in wet oasis with fresh flowers because they will become mouldy.) Similarly, make sure that moss is quite dry if you are wiring dried flowers on to it.

Australian Arrangement

This simple vase arrangement of long-lasting but expensive flowers has an Australian flavour, combining flowering eucalyptus with an exotic variety known as "Kangaroo paws". Striking, but not over-dramatic, this display would look comfortable in many different types of setting.

FLOWERS AND FOLIAGE

Flowering eucalyptus
"Kangaroo paws"
Ivy

MATERIALS

Vase

METHOD

1   Fill the vase with water. Add eucalyptus around the rim of the vase so that stems cross, providing a support.
2   Balance the taller "Kangaroo paws" in the centre of the vase, inserting between the crossed eucalyptus stems.
3   Add the ivy trails to one side.

CARE

This display is very long-lasting. Change the water from time to time.

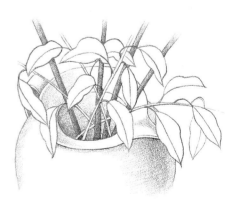

Silvery Display

This low arrangement is both an economical and effective way of using a few flowers. Here one open stem of lilies has been combined with foliage and buds cut from a silver leaf cyclamen plant which was past its best.

FLOWERS AND FOLIAGE

Silver leaf cyclamen
White 'Casablanca' lilies

MATERIALS

Low bowl

METHOD

1   Trim leaves and remaining buds from plant, leaving as much stem length as possible.
2   Begin at the outer rim of the bowl, laying the leaves around the edge and gradually building up towards the centre.
3   Insert cyclamen buds towards the edge of the bowl.
4   Rest two open lily heads on the leaves at the centre.

CARE

Change the water in the bowl after several days. The display is long-lasting.

Three in a Row

The stylized form of protea flowers has been exploited by a simple alcove display, using a glass trough filled with moss. This naive effect, designed to look as if flowers are growing, emphasizes their childlike quality.

FLOWERS AND FOLIAGE

Three protea
Bun moss

MATERIALS

Glass trough
Oasis

METHOD

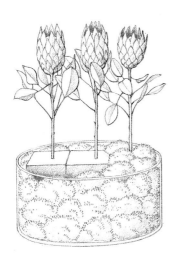

1   Line the trough with bun moss. Fill with wet oasis, cut level with the rim of the trough.
2   Insert the protea at regular intervals, pushing down firmly so that the heavy heads are supported. Cover the oasis with more bun moss.

CARE

Top up with water to prolong the life of the flowers and keep the moss green. Pour the water slowly to avoid getting a water line. This display will last two to three weeks.

Fruit Baskets

A centrepiece for a buffet table or sideboard, this arrangement of descending baskets, filled with fruit and vegetables, is crowned by a fan of rushes and grasses. The rushes can be changed from time to time.

FLOWERS AND FOLIAGE

Fruit
Gourds
Moss
Grasses and rushes

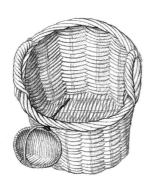

MATERIALS

Baskets
Wire
Vase

METHOD

1   Put the grasses and rushes into a narrow-necked vase filled with water and place in a basket.
2   Bind wire around the handles of smaller baskets and push the wires through the weave of the large basket. Twist the wires inside the larger basket so that the smaller ones are held firm.
3   Fill the small baskets with fruit and gourds.
4   Pack the gap between the vase and large basket with moss.

CARE

Change the water in the vase.

Contemporary Design

The spare, clean lines of this modern interior demand a display which is equally stark and striking. Here the lichen-covered container relates to the gunmetal leather upholstery, while red dogwood branches provide a subtle touch of colour.

FLOWERS AND FOLIAGE

Dogwood branches (*Cornus alba*)
Moss
Lichen
Ivy

MATERIALS

Bucket
String
Wire

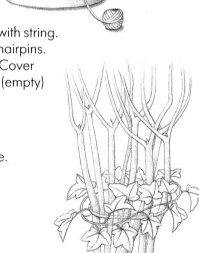

METHOD

1 Bind moss on to the outside of the bucket with string.
2 Pin lichen clumps over the moss with wire hairpins.
3 Bunch twigs together, binding with string. Cover string with a trail of ivy. Place dogwood in (empty) bucket and trail ivy over the edge.

CARE

No care is required as the display is water free.

New Look

Carnations can be dull, especially when they are arranged in a vase with asparagus fern. To revamp their image, combine with more exotic foliage, such as these begonia leaves, and cut low to display the heads fully. Begonia leaves are available from good florists or you can cut up a straggly pot plant which is past its best.

FLOWERS AND FOLIAGE

10 to 12 'Clove' carnations
Rosehips
Begonia rex leaves

MATERIALS

Low bowl, about 6-7 in (15-18 cm) deep.

METHOD

1   Place begonia leaves around the edge of a bowl filled with water.
2   Lay stems of rosehips on top.
3   Gather the heads of carnations together in a dome. Cut stems level so that the heads appear just above the edge of the vase. Rest on leaves.
4   Add a few odd stems of rosehips in among the carnations.

CARE

Due to the begonia leaves this display is not very long-lasting. Change water regularly.

Dried Roses

If you plan ahead, you can begin drying flowers in the summer months to ensure a supply to take you through the fall and winter. This medieval-style cluster of roses is easy to make, portable and simple to maintain. Since it is circular and not flat-backed, it will suit a variety of locations.

FLOWERS AND FOLIAGE

Dried roses

MATERIALS

String
Tasselled cord

METHOD

1 Bind bunches of approximately 10 flowers at a time with string.
2 Arrange bunches in a circular fashion, about a central bunch, binding each in with string as it is added.
3 Cover the twine with a tasselled cord. Cut stems level.

CARE

The roses can become more fragile in hot rooms. Handle with care.

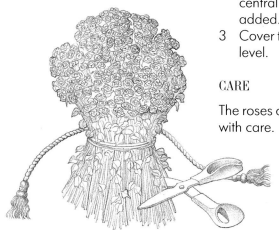

Shades of Blue

Easy on the eye and pleasant to live with, this early fall display relies on a mixture of subtle shades of blue. The low, full vase is not easily upset, ideal for an area which is in constant use. Hydrangea heads, which deepen in colour in the fall, taking on burgundy tinges, make useful fillers when flowers are scarce.

FLOWERS AND FOLIAGE

Hydrangea
Scabious
Eryngium thistle
Heather

MATERIALS

Low round vase

METHOD

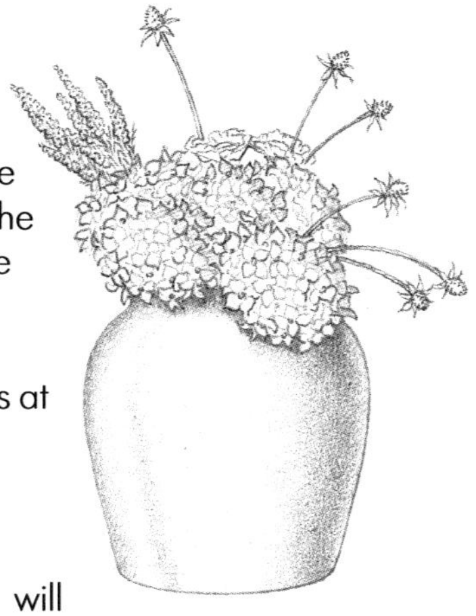

1 Cut the hydrangea stems so that heads rest on the rim of the vase. Place heads around the edge of the vase, so that they form a support for the rest of the flowers.
2 Insert the remainder of the flowers between the hydrangea heads. Cluster species and cut groups at different lengths to create a dome effect.

CARE

Change water as often as possible. Flower food will prolong the life of this display.

Indian Summer

Echoes of summer warmth are displayed in this late summer/early fall mixture of pinks and yellows, set in a sunny spot beside two wicker chairs. Flower colours tone with upholstery and china; the basket container coordinates with the style of furniture.

FLOWERS AND FOLIAGE

Marigolds
Azalea, cut from a pot plant
Phlox
Achillea
Honeysuckle
Miniature roses
Jasmine foliage

MATERIALS

Basket
Plastic lining
Oasis

METHOD

1 Line the basket with plastic and fill with wet oasis to a height of 3-4 in (8-10 cm) above rim.
2 Insert the highest foliage. Place trails of jasmine and honeysuckle out to each corner and from the centre front down.
3 Fill in empty areas with foliage.
4 Insert a group of marigolds at the centre top; to the right place a cluster of azalea.
5 Place stems of phlox at one edge, miniature roses and achillea at the other.
6 Fill with the remainder of flowers to make an uneven, rambling look.

CARE

Water daily, spraying occasionally with a plant spray. The arrangement will last about a week.

Dried Garland

A garland composed entirely of dried flowers and foliage hangs across a fine gilt mirror, the depth of colour and richness of content echoing the splendour of the setting. The asymmetric design helps to tone down the grandeur.

FLOWERS AND FOLIAGE

Dried helichrysum
Dried amaranthus
Dried heather
Mixture of dried foliage and leaves
Sphagnum moss

MATERIALS

Chickenwire
Wire

METHOD

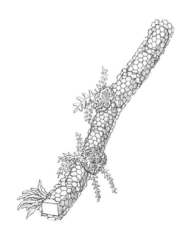

1. Wrap clumps of moss in chickenwire to make a long sausage shape, securing the sides with wire.
2. Group flowers and foliage in small bunches, securing with wire, using double leg mount method (see page 33).
3. Insert flowers, starting at the outer edges. Fill in to the centre, building round in an arc.
4. Hook the garland in place using wire or string loops.

CARE

When the garland becomes dusty, clean gently with a hairdryer. Lasts indefinitely.

Fall Weddings

For a really memorable fall wedding, as distinct from a wedding which just happens to take place in the fall it is important to acknowledge the season and express its unique atmosphere and characteristics. I always feel that it is a pity to plan weddings without any regard or reference to the time of year in which they are celebrated. Seasonal decorations, particularly flowers, can give a wedding day a special theme which unifies and enhances the occasion.

The seasonal approach is also practical. Just as a wedding dress with a deep décolleté or an off-the-shoulder design in fine silk, lace or tulle would be uncomfortably chilly on a cold, blustery fall day, flowers which are out of season are both expensive and inappropriate. Even if there is a strong family tradition or sentimental reason for choosing a variety or shade of flower which is at odds with the fall mood, it is far better to reconsider and choose an alternative which is more in keeping with the season. For example, the pastels which are more typical of the spring and summer range are both costly and lacking in impact on gloomy days. Many fall flowers hold up well in wedding arrangements; in addition, there is the option of using dried flowers for an original and seasonal display.

Above left: For a fall bride, a head circlet of rosehips, ivy, Virginia creeper, bun moss and anemones. Warm shades complement the complexion on cold, grey days.

Right: Deep pink is the colour theme for this fall bouquet, which features a large central amaryllis trumpet, azalea, rosehips, skimmia, ivy and Virginia creeper.

Left: A chuppah *is a natural focal point and should be decorated to create maximum impact. Here cascades of hops and roses in different shades of peach tumble from the four corners of the canopy.*

CHOOSING WEDDING FLOWERS

Although there are few problems with overheating or wilting in the fall, certain flowers will simply not last well in bouquets or headdresses if they are wired. A bouquet can take an hour and a half to make and must often be delivered to the bride at least two hours before the wedding so that there is enough time for the hairdresser and photographer to do their work. This means that by the time the wedding party is ready for the ceremony, the flowers will already have been out of water for nearly four hours. Appropriate flowers are best chosen in consultation with a florist, who will be able to advise on suitability.

I am often asked how to preserve a bouquet as a keepsake. Many bouquets can be successfully dried by immersing them in silica gel (crystals) (page 33). An alternative is to opt for a dried flower bouquet which is particularly relevant in autumn. All of the dried flowers listed on page 31 are suitable for wedding work.

SUITABLE (FRESH) FALL FLOWERS AND FOLIAGE

Alstroemeria   Delicate, expensive and exotic looking, but relatively cheap and long-lasting, even wired.
Amaryllis   Dramatic and resilient. Large trumpets.
Anemone   If treated with care, can be wired.
Carnation   Cheap, long-lasting and perfumed. "Shatter" the large blooms to use wired in segments.
Chrysanthemum   Single variety blooms in apricot, bronze, gold are very effective.
Elaeagnus   Good silvery or gold foliage.
Euphorbia   Similar to orange blossom. Useful trails for bouquets.
Freesia   Ever-popular wedding flower. Wonderful scent.
Gerbera   Large, daisy-like flower.
Gladiolus   Individual florets can be wired in bouquets.
Heather   White heather is a traditional symbol of good luck.
Hebe   Good wedding foliage.
Ivy   Invaluable as foliage or trails.
Lily   Trumpets or star-like blooms available in a variety of colours.
Love-lies-bleeding   Dramatic, modern style.
Ranunculus   Luscious, old-fashioned country flower; good at giving sense of movement.
Rose   Use warm, fall shades.
Skimmia   Golden or red variety both equally effective.
Viburnum   Pinky floret can be useful in bouquets.
Virginia creeper   Trails of red foliage give a rich, fall look.

THE BRIDE'S FLOWERS

When planning wedding flowers today, we naturally concentrate on style and suitability. But, traditionally, the flowers that were carried by the bride were selected for their meaning as much as their appearance. Particularly significant were flowers which symbolized fertility. One way of making a wedding special and original is to break away from modern conventions and revive such traditions and associations from the past. The present-day popularity of roses and gypsophila in wedding bouquets, for example, is really based on no more than convenience: both flowers are readily available year-round. Yet however beautiful a posy of roses and gypsophila may be, this combination has simply been seen too often. Investigating seasonal varieties brings freshness to the occasion and expresses a strong connection with the world of nature.

In the fall, the theme is ripeness and abundance. In the past, wheat garlands, symbolizing fertility, were the standard accompaniment of the bride, a tradition that could well be revived for fall weddings. Fruit and even vegetables can be combined with flowers in a bouquet: a strand of berries is as decorative as jasmine or honeysuckle; purple-veined cabbage leaves are as stunning as any exotic florist's foliage. Scarlet-tinted trails of Virginia creeper create a sense of fall richness, while filled baskets carried through the crook of the arm pursue the harvest theme. Even chestnuts can be incorporated into headdresses and bouquets. When combining fruit or berries with flowers in a bouquet, make sure that they cannot be easily crushed, to avoid staining the wedding dress.

Dried flower bouquets can help to emphasize a Victorian theme. Dried flowers are not fluid enough for trailing bouquets, but lend themselves to compact designs, such as circlets, posies, garlands and pomanders. They work well with heavier fabrics, such as brocades and velvets.

In practical terms, it is best to develop ideas for the bride's flowers first. The bride is the focus of attention throughout the day and it is vital that her flowers suit her

Right: Dried flowers have a strong nostalgic appeal. This headdress and posy are composed of dried roses, peonies, helichrysum, copper beech foliage and nigella (love-in-a-mist) seedheads.

personality and style. This means taking into account her colouring, height and size – as well as her wishes. But, above all, it means planning the flowers to suit the style of the wedding dress. Bouquets and headdresses should always be discussed after the dress is designed or chosen.

In the fall, bridal wear should be made of warmer fabric, such as brocades, velvets or textured silks. At the very least, a thin dress should be accompanied by a wrap or jacket which can be worn whenever the bride is out of doors – getting to the church or being photographed, for example. Similarly, flower colours should reinforce the sense of warmth. Cool whites or blues do not complement most peoples' complexions on a grey day. Choose coral rather than red, ivory rather than pure white, gold rather than primrose yellow, and avoid blue as a dominant shade.

FLOWERS FOR THE ATTENDANTS

The bride's flowers should set the theme for all the wedding decorations: wide differences of colour, design, or type of flower could easily result in visual chaos. When it comes to selecting flowers for the attendants, versions of the bridal bouquet are often most suitable. Subtle variations on the same theme are perfectly acceptable, but not an outright clash of styles.

For adult bridesmaids, a smaller and less elaborate bouquet, based on the design of the bride's flowers, is often the best solution. Male family members might like to choose a flower from the bride's bouquet for their buttonholes: at any rate, try to avoid the stale and standard solution of carnations. Women can wear corsages incorporating some of the bridal flowers.

I particularly enjoy seeing little bridesmaids and pages at a wedding. Here, coordination with the bride is less important. Although it is undoubtedly more successful if the same type and colours of flower are used, designs for children can and really should be different. Children need flowers which are fun to carry, easy to manage and which are tailored to suit them. Tiny baskets, pomanders, garlands, hoops and posies are all intriguing and add a touch of whimsy and delight.

FLOWERS FOR THE CEREMONY

Since the fall flower range is rather limited, when it comes to decorating a large space such as a church or synagogue, the main problem is how to be effective and original without spending a fortune on imported or commercially grown flowers. The solution, in most cases, is to rely more heavily on foliage, nuts, berries, grasses and other fall fruits and vegetables. Leaves, in particular, are a richly decorative element, both cheap and colourful. Copper beech, golden oak and brilliant maple leaves are every bit as eyecatching as the most expensive hothouse blooms. They can be used as a substitute for floral displays or strewn along the aisle to make a path of colour. Again, picking up on the fertility theme, hops, wheatsheaves and boughs laden with apples or berries will all create an original impact.

Above left: The green tassels of love-lies-bleeding lend an exotic touch to a child's circlet composed of miniature yellow roses, ivy and rosehips.

Right: Candles, bright red ribbon and a large country basket make useful accessories in the fall when the range of affordable flowers is small. Astilbes, hydrangea and blackberries bring out the rich shades of the church interior.

As far as flowers are concerned, chrysanthemums are reliable, inexpensive and long-lasting: the ultimate filler. But they need not be dull and clichéd. The secret is to select single varieties (those which resemble daisies) and assemble them in graduated mixtures with the deeper colours recessed in the arrangement: for example, gold and bronze, dusty pink and red.

Similarly, carnations are not the most exotic of flowers and their stiff straight stems often prevent them from looking in any way natural. But their range of colours, sweet perfume, low cost and availability mean that they are hard to overlook. To make a more interesting display with carnations, or indeed any flower which is safe and expected, combine them with more exotic foliage. In the case of carnations, avoid asparagus fern and cupressus at all costs; opt instead for begonia leaves (very effective with red carnations), cyclamen (for smaller arrangements), or eucalyptus (for white displays).

Candles can also be a useful supplement. The flickering light creates a sense of mystery in dark interiors and the base of the candles can be given a simple floral treatment, which is an effective way of using few flowers. If the budget is very limited, reserve your best efforts to one or two large displays, positioned where they will have most impact and visibility – at the altar and at the entrance. Pew end decorations can be simple – and free – displays of foliage.

FLOWERS FOR THE RECEPTION

Many of the same points apply when it comes to decorations for the reception. Leaves, for example, can look stunning trimming buffet or drinks tables, especially if the idea is carried through to the presentation of food. Or you can combine food and flowers by filling edible leaves such as *lollo rosso* or purple cabbage, with open rose heads to create an exotic centrepiece.

Flowers and foliage can be entwined with swathes of fabric which complements the material in the bride's or bridesmaid's dresses. Fabric is a dramatic, luxurious alternative to ribbon and also has the advantage of taking up space so that fewer flowers are needed.

If you plan well ahead, favourite flowers from the summer garden can be dried and set aside for a wedding later in the year – a solution which is both economical and meaningful. Dried flowers particularly suit designs such as garlands which can be used to wind down stairways or frame an entrance.

At a reception, as at any party, displays should be large enough to be seen from afar, with flowers grouped in clusters of three or more to increase visibility. Avoid floor-level arrangements, which will only be obstructive and overlooked and remember to concentrate on decorating the key positions – entrances, the main tables and around the cake – all places where photographs are likely to be taken.

Right: A pedestal arrangement for the front of the church has more flower content than the pew end display. Red antirrhinums, pink chrysanthemums and heather have been added to the berries and foliages.

Tied Bouquet

The colouring is what gives this bouquet its sophistication. The style, however, is simple and natural, a design suitable for holding in the crook of the arm. This type of bouquet suits wedding dresses with full, flowing skirts.

FLOWERS AND FOLIAGE

Heather
Astilbe
Hydrangea
Viburnum
'Blue Moon' roses
Oak leaves

MATERIALS

String
Ribbon

METHOD

1 Begin with the central rose. Attach string about 8 in (20 cm) down the stem. (The further down the stem you attach the string, the larger the bouquet can be.)
2 Add hydrangeas and large leaves, turning the bunch in your hand and binding each flower in with string.
3 Edge with the daintier flowers of heather and astilbe.
4 Cut stems level. Cover the string with ribbon.

CARE

The bouquet will last well all day, particularly if refreshed by a drink of water.

Candlelight

Decorating a large area can be expensive, especially in the fall when flowers are scarce. As a substitute for filling the church with flowers, candles can generate a great sense of atmosphere. The bases can be trimmed with a few inexpensive flowers in rich colours.

FLOWERS AND FOLIAGE

Violets
Miniature red roses
Winter-flowering
pansies, potted
Large dark green ivy leaves
Bun moss

MATERIALS

Candle
Oasis
Saucer
Cottonwool
Heavy-gauge
florist's wire
Waterproof tape

METHOD

1 Make two hairpins out of heavy-gauge florist's wire and bind on to the candle with waterproof tape.
2 Anchor candle in soaked oasis, placed on a saucer.
3 Position pot of pansies to the rear, covering the pot with moss.
4 Insert the ivy leaves into oasis, together with cluster of roses.
5 Wrap stems of violets in damp cottonwool. Lay both bunches under ivy leaves, so that flowers protrude.

CARE

This arrangement can be made the day before the wedding.

Hanging Decoration

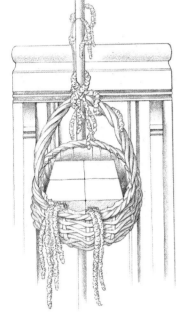

Most pew-end decorations are designed to either "grow" up from the floor or down from the top of the pew; this variation is a hanging basket. Fruit and vegetables, as well as dried and fresh flowers, create a harvest festival atmosphere.

FLOWERS AND FOLIAGE	MATERIALS
Dried love-lies-bleeding	Basket
Miniature red roses	Plastic lining
Celosia	Wire
Aubergines	Oasis
Figs	Sticks or short
Cranberries or red currants	lengths of cane

METHOD

1 Line the basket with plastic and fill with wet oasis to a height of 6 in (15 cm) above rim. Wire basket handle on to the pew end.
2 Insert love-lies-bleeding in the bottom right-hand corner to overspill the basket. Twist more love-lies-bleeding over the handle and up to hide the wire or hook.
3 Cluster miniature roses at the base of the central love-lies-bleeding. Group celosia over love-lies-bleeding at bottom right and to the left of the basket.
4 Wire aubergines and figs on to sticks and insert in remaining gaps of oasis. Sprinkle berries here and there.

CARE

This display will last a week if required.

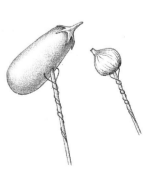

68

Fall Cascade

A tumbling cascade of hops and open roses twining around a pillar creates a dramatic focal point in a synagogue, visible both from the floor and balcony levels. In a large area, it is better to concentrate efforts on two or three important positions than spread the budget too thinly.

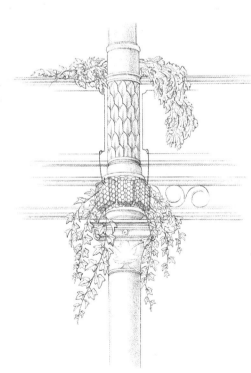

FLOWERS AND FOLIAGE

Hops or any other creeper
Ivy
Roses

MATERIALS

Oasis
Chickenwire
Wire
Hooks
Waterproof tape

METHOD

1. Wrap blocks of wet oasis in chickenwire. Attach to pillar by binding with waterproof tape. Insert hooks into the wire and secure on balustrade.
2. Drape garlands of hops from the oasis up and over the balcony rail. Attach with wire and allow to fall back down as if growing. Insert and wire stands of hops at the base of the oasis and twine them round the pillar.
3. Cover the oasis with trails of ivy.
4. Insert masses of roses at all angles to create the effect of a bush.
5. Cut a few rose heads short and wire on to the trails of creeper.

Church Gate

A bright and cheerful garland of fall flowers creates a welcome at a country church gate. You can gather almost any available flower, in any colour, making a virtue out of fall limitations. This type of garland is simple and quick to do.

FLOWERS AND FOLIAGE

Marigolds
Anemones
Heather
Violets
Ivy

MATERIALS

String

METHOD

1   Take a strand of ivy and bind with string on to another length of string. Gradually add flowers and foliage, binding every inch or so.
2   Drape garlands into position, attaching with knots of string.

CARE

This garland will only last for the day as flowers are out of water.

Special Occasions

Many fall celebrations are inextricably bound up with nature. The central occasions of Thanksgiving in North America and the various harvest festivals and fêtes in Europe mark the end of the growing season, when the rewards of a summer of hard work are reaped. Traditional festivities underline a natural instinct for gathering and storing the produce of the year to act as a reserve for winter months. For any fall celebration — from a dinner party to a Guy Fawkes bonfire, it is particularly satisfying to make use of these harvest images and time-honoured symbols.

Left: Harvest festival is an occasion for the simple enjoyment of natural things: country produce, homemade bread, cottage flowers.

Right: A bold table centre with very limited flower content consists of red roses supplemented by turnips, lichen, moss and dogwood twigs.

Left: Wreaths can be used to decorate walls, doors, tables or furniture. A mossed wreath frame has been used here as the basis for a display of nuts, moss, dried roses, twigs and pebbles (attached with a glue gun).

Right: Nothing could be more evocative of fall than a simple wheatsheaf, bound with string and tied with a plait of wheat stems.

PARTY FLOWERS

At this time of year, despite the chill in the air and the increasing likelihood of poor weather, many parties nevertheless have an outdoor theme. A Hallowe'en fancy dress party or a Guy Fawkes firework display provide the opportunity for a bonfire and one last barbecue; earlier in the season it may well be warm enough to consider a picnic lunch outdoors. Flower arrangements can help to promote a sense of occasion and make the event something special.

Displays designed for the garden should never be formal. Humble containers such as terracotta pots, stone urns and rustic baskets are unpretentious and look as if they belong. Arrangements are best if they are low and solid constructions, with no extended lines: in the fall the aim is to create a sense of warmth and security. Asters and button chrysanthemums have the right country look; lilies or anthuriums, for example, would be just too sophisticated. Combinations of fruit, nuts, vegetables and flowers are particularly effective, especially if the arrangement incorporates food which is intended to be eaten. In this context, it is worth repeating the warning that if you do gather berries please check that they are harmless. Many of the brightest and most attractive berries — which are especially appealing to children — are poisonous, some lethally so.

In many countries a dried arrangement of grasses, flowers or gourds was traditionally pinned up over the entrance to the house in the fall to ward off evil spirits and protect the occupants. Nowadays, door decorations provide a friendly way of announcing a party or special event. At the simplest, a wheatsheaf, made of a handful of wheat stems braided together, can be reminiscent of the more intricate corn dolly. If you have apple trees, windfalls can be used to make an apple wreath for a birthday or Hallowe'en party — more original than tying balloons to the door knocker. A ring of terracotta pots can be mounted on a wreath base and filled with "treats" for Hallowe'en tricksters. And for children, there is nothing more exciting than a row of fierce-looking jack o'lanterns winking in the window.

TABLE SETTINGS

All table settings should be low so as not to obstruct views or inhibit conversation. Large flowers cut low, naturally trailing species that wind the length of the table and tiny posies at each place setting are all ways of providing table-level interest without interference. It is also worth remembering that heavily scented flowers may inhibit your appreciation of food and wine.

A table decoration for Thanksgiving can be based on the idea of a cornucopia, with a mixture of flowers and fruit spilling out across the table from small pots or baskets resting on their sides. Pheasant's feathers can be combined with strands of berries and rich fall flowers to accompany a dinner party which features game. Rosehips, sedum, ivy and chrysanthemums can be used to supplement the more expensive roses, euphorbia and azalea.

Displays in the shape of trees add theatricality and a certain splendour to a formal occasion. The solidity of the form is in keeping with the fall mood. "Trees" can be composed of dried flowers or foliages and placed in front of a mirror or flanking a buffet table.

GIFTS

Flowers make perfect presents, especially in situations where a more personal gift would be inappropriate. However, this does not mean that they should be impersonal themselves. With a little thought and effort, and perhaps some advice from a florist, it is possible to make a selection which reflects the personality or style of the recipient.

As a thank-you present or to take to a dinner party, spiralled or tied bunches are particularly welcome. Tied bunches are also a good choice for hospital visits, but avoid perfumed flowers as a heavy scent can be overwhelming. Dried flower arrangements, similarly, need no care and last much longer than a fresh display.

Flowers also combine well with other presents: with grapes and Beaujolais Nouveau for a celebration; with a soft toy for a new baby; with chocolates or champagne for a birthday or anniversary.

Left: Moss and miniature dried roses are set off with lavish twists of white muslin in this striking wreath used as a table centre.

Right: An exercise in coordination. A collection of garden flowers – sedum, chrysanthemum and rosehips – supplemented by roses and euphorbia from the florist, pick out the colours in the dinner service.

Apple Wreath

A door decoration for any fall party – Thanksgiving, Hallowe'en or Guy Fawkes – this wreath uses readily available windfall apples mounted on a wispy scarecrow frame of moss. The different colours of apples provide variety: it is important not to strive for perfection.

FLOWERS AND FOLIAGE

Apples
Wheat
Moss

MATERIALS

Metal wreath frame
Wire
String

METHOD

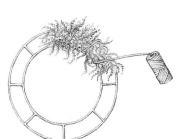

1 Bind clumps of moss onto the wreath frame, using string. Bind loosely, allowing moss to straggle.
2 Insert a wire through an apple. Pull both ends of the wire down and twist together. Insert the wires into the moss and through, doubling back to hold the apple firm. Repeat all around the frame.
3 Bunch the wheat in sheaves and bind in the same manner as the apples. Cover the wire with a strand of wheat, insert into the wreath, through the apples.

CARE

The wreath will last three to four weeks if kept in a cool environment.

Rose Tree

A dramatic decoration for a party or an ideal gift, this rose tree is a subtle combination of roses, honeysuckle and jasmine, sedum and moss. Colours are soft and gentle; content is not very expensive. A miniature version could be made for a dining table.

FLOWERS AND FOLIAGE

Honeysuckle
Jasmine flowers and trails
Roses
Sedum
Moss

MATERIALS

Basket
Pot
Oasis
Waterproof tape
Florist's wire
Log
Quick-drying cement

METHOD

1   Cement the log into the pot. Place it in the basket and pack around the outside with moss. Attach oasis to the top of the log with waterproof tape.
2   Cover parts of the oasis by pinning moss and sedum, cut low, with hairpins of florist's wire. Insert trails of jasmine and honeysuckle.
3   Insert large open roses at the centre, smaller buds to the outer edge.

CARE

Water oasis carefully to prolong life.

Wicker Wreath

Terracotta pots, attached to a robust wicker wreath, can be filled with a variety of items, depending on the nature of the occasion; treats for Hallowe'en, little toys or sweets for a birthday party, or apples, as here, for a seasonal look.

FLOWERS AND FOLIAGE

Apples
Strands of berries
Moss

MATERIALS

Wicker wreath
Terracotta plant pots
Wire
Ribbon

METHOD

1   Poke moss between the strands of wicker and bind on with wire. Add a small pad of moss on top of wicker and again wire in place.
2   Insert heavy-gauge wire through the drainage hole in pot and over the pot's edge, twisting ends together. Insert wire through the moss pad and double back to secure.
3   Group pots together and fill with apples.
4   Tie on ribbon and bind on strands of berries.

CARE

Replace items in filling pots as necessary.

Game Table

Pheasant's feathers trail across the table in a rich, fall display which combines flowers such as dahlias with apples, moss and driftwood. Inspiration for this type of tableau can be gained by looking at paintings, such as Dutch still lifes.

FLOWERS AND FOLIAGE

Dahlias
Cotoneaster
Moss
Ivy
Berries
Fruit
Rosehips

MATERIALS

Oasis
Copper bowl
Driftwood
Pheasant's feathers

METHOD

1   Fill the bowl with oasis to 3 in (8 cm) above the rim. Insert feathers at an upward angle so that they trail down on to the table. Add ivy and berries in the same manner.
2   Wire the fruit onto sticks and insert into the oasis.
3   Gradually build up with flowers, fruit and driftwood, working from the base up to the highest point.

CARE

Water oasis to prolong flower life.

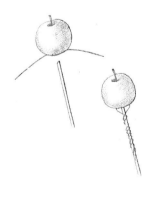

Impromptu Table Setting

Ivy, hydrangea heads and trailing foliage are the only elements required for this impulsive, last-minute display. The ingredients are simply laid on the table, twining around each place setting. Nothing could be simpler to do or more effective.

FLOWERS AND FOLIAGE

Hydrangea heads
Ivy
Trailing foliage

MATERIALS

Candelabra

METHOD

1   Lay strands of trailing foliage along the table, between place settings, leading away from the candelabra.
2   Twine the foliage around the stem of the candelabra. Place hydrangea heads towards the centre of the table, covering the places where the foliage strands join.

CARE

As the display is out of water, it will only last a short time.

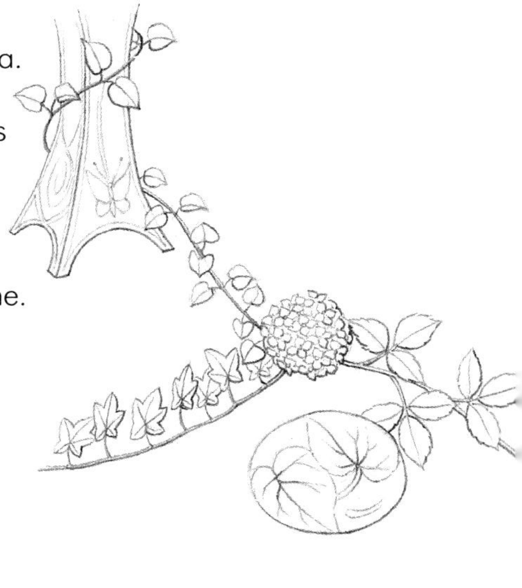

Outdoor Party

Chrysanthemums look their best used in an original, unexpected way: here massed in a vase and combined with baskets full of apples. The bright colours have a rustic look and show up well in the golden fall light.

FLOWERS AND FOLIAGE

Chrysanthemums
Oak foliage
Rosehips
Apples
Moss

MATERIALS

Baskets
Vase
Wire

METHOD

1 Mass the heads of the chrysanthemums together and cut the stems level. Place the flowers in a narrow vase, put it into the largest basket and fill the gap between the two containers with moss.
2 Attach apples by inserting a wire through, twisting ends together and pushing the wire into the moss. Cluster apples on the basket rim.
3 Gather baskets together at the base of the larger basket and fill with fruit and foliage until overflowing.

CARE

Ensure vase of chrysanthemums is full of water, change water when necessary.

Apple Harvest

Apples are the focal point of this display, which also includes ranunculus, camellia leaves and ivy. Inspired by and commemorating the fruit harvest, this basket is an ideal decoration for an outdoor lunch, but would work equally well indoors.

FLOWERS AND FOLIAGE

Apples
Ivy
Camellia foliage
Ranunculus

MATERIALS

Basket
Plastic lining
Oasis
Sticks

METHOD

1   Line the basket with plastic and fill with wet oasis. Cover the oasis with foliage. Insert ivy trails at an upward angle so that they trail over the edge of the basket.
2   Push apples on to short sticks and insert into the oasis in clusters.
3   Add flowers towards the trails of ivy.

CARE

Water oasis daily to prolong flower life.

Table Garland

Everyone has a good view of the display when it consists of a garland winding the length of the dining table. The garland can be arranged to weave a path through serving dishes; it need not be very wide. Pine cones bring out the natural tones of the wood.

FLOWERS AND FOLIAGE

Fruit
Cones
Moss
Heather

MATERIALS

Plastic lining
Chickenwire
Wire

METHOD

1 Wrap small clumps of moss in chickenwire to make a long sausage shape. Pin plastic along the base to protect the table from damp.
2 Wire cones and fruit, twisting the ends of the wire together and inserting into the moss in groups.
3 Insert clusters of heather interspersed between the fruit. Hairpin bun moss to fill gaps, using wire.

CARE

No care is needed as fruit, cones and moss will not benefit from extra moisture.

Asparagus Basket

The edible outnumbers the inedible in a compact, structured display incorporating a host of seasonal fruits and vegetables, all tumbling from an asparagus "basket". This type of rather extravagant arrangement is quite time-consuming to construct and is really designed for a very special occasion.

FLOWERS AND FOLIAGE

Grapes
Pomegranate
Red cauliflower
Plums
Red potatoes
Asparagus
Ivy
Skimmia flowers
Azalea (potted)
Roses

MATERIALS

Plate
Oasis (two)
Wire

METHOD

1 Place oasis on a dinner plate, cutting one block at a sloping angle. Hairpin asparagus around the oasis in a fence-like arrangement, using wire.
2 Place ivy at the base to cover the plate. Pin grapes on to spill over the plate.
3 Gradually build up the fruit and vegetables, securing with wire.
4 Insert flowers and cut azalea flower to cover any remaining exposed areas of oasis.

CARE

Water sparingly to prolong flower life. Keep in a cool environment if possible.

Classical Urn

This sumptuous combination of fruit, vegetable and flowers, trimmed with a velvet bow, has a certain period style displayed in a classical urn. The position of the urn, in front of a gilt mirror, maximises its impact. The arrangement is very long-lasting and worth the extra effort and expense.

FLOWERS AND FOLIAGE

Skimmia
Roses
Bun moss
Lichen
Onions
Swedes
Pomegranates
Pine cones

MATERIALS

Urn
Oasis
Chickenwire
Canes
Wire
Velvet bow

METHOD

1 Build up blocks of oasis in the urn to the required shape. Cover with chickenwire.
2 Begin at the top, inserting daintier varieties, such as skimmia foliage. Work downwards, inserting fruit, vegetables and cones as well as flowers.
3 Wrap wire around cones and twist ends together; insert wooden canes into fruit, push wire through and wrap around canes.
4 Fill the gaps with moss and lichen, hairpinned into position. Pin velvet bow in place.

CARE

This arrangement is very long-lasting. Water oasis to prolong life of flowers and foliage.

Basic Techniques

All cut flowers will last longer if they are properly trimmed and conditioned before arranging; some species have special needs in this respect. In addition, there are various simple techniques, widely used by florists, which can extend the creative scope. One word of caution: wiring flowers for bouquets and headdresses is a specialist skill and requires training.

Left: The font in a country church is an ideal place for a harvest festival display.

Right: A wicker chair overgrown with trails of ivy and fern makes an unusual but highly effective arrangement.

CUTTING AND CONDITIONING

Most flowers will need to be trimmed once you have arrived home. The area of the stem presented to the water should be fresh – stem ends which have been out of water for any length of time tend to dry up and absorb water less efficiently.

It is a good idea to trim at least ½-1 inch (1-2 cm) from the stems, more if the arrangement requires. Cut the stems at an oblique angle so that the largest surface area possible is available to take up the water.

Once the stems have been trimmed, put the flowers into a deep bucket of water for two hours so a reservoir can be taken up into the heads. This is especially important if the flowers will be used long-stemmed. The same advice applies equally to flowers cut from the garden or pot plants.

SPECIAL CARE

Woody stems
The stems of certain flowers such as chrysanthemums, viburnum, cotoneaster and flowering foliages are fibrous and woody. To aid uptake of water, hammer the stems so they split and splinter.

Roses
Most roses come wrapped in plastic lining and the heads may have wilted or dropped slightly by the time you get them home. Remove the plastic lining and take off the thorns from the stems so that the flowers are more comfortable to work with. Trim the stems with a sharp knife (they do not need to be hammered) and dip them into 2 inches (5 cm) of boiling water for 20 seconds to clear any airblocks. Then wrap the flowers in tissue paper or newspaper and place in deep water for two hours. Some of the foliage can be left on the stems to aid water absorption.

Gerbera
If stems are soft and limp, they will stiffen in water, but stiffen into a bent shape. Support upright if you want straight stems.

Celosia

This flower stains the water, according to the flower colour, so avoid using in clear containers.

Euphorbia

Stems are sealed prior to sale. If you need to recut stems, they should be resealed by holding in a flame so that sap does not leak out.

Left: Vibrant clashing shades of orange, pink and red make an eye-catching display. Amaryllis, poppies and alstroemeria are supplemented by rosehips and ivy.

WATER

Cool water will prolong the life of cut flowers. In some circumstances, however, you may wish to place the flowers in warm water to open buds.

The water should be as deep as the container allows. The crucial relationshp is between the length of the stem and depth of the water: the longer the stem, the deeper the water should be. Long-stemmed flowers in shallow containers will last a fraction of their normal lifespan.

Water is an alien medium for flowers; stems drown and decompose, depositing particles which change the chemical nature of the water. To slow down the process of decay, take off the foliage below the water line and change the water in containers as frequently as possible, retrimming the stems by ½ inch (1 cm) at each water change. You can also add a flower food to the water which will make the flowers last longer, but as this yellows the water it is best not used in see-through containers. With flower food, you can change the water every three to four days; without, allow only one or two days between changes. And the warmer the weather, the quicker the water will need changing.

One of the problems of needing to change the water frequently is that you run the risk of disturbing a carefully composed and balanced arrangement. If the flowers are all in good condition, you can stand the vase or container under the tap and leave the water running until it has come up over the side. But if some of the flowers are beginning to brown, changing the water provides an opportunity to discard dead and drying heads, retrim the stems of those which survive and rearrange, perhaps in a different container. In mixed arrangements, some species will last longer than others and this is a good way of gaining maximum value and enjoyment. Similarly, flowers in bud can be arranged in a tall, elegant container; once opened, they can be cut and arranged in a lower vase to display the heads prominently.

Always clean containers thoroughly between use. Use bleach or a washing-up liquid and scour to remove the tidemark of algae and scum. Dirty containers only speed up the process of decay.

Right: Dusty pink chrysanthemums and amaryllis trumpets make a floor-level display, the glass cube containers echoing the effect of the glass brick screen.

TEMPERATURE

In general, flowers do best positioned where they will not be subject to extremes of temperature.

Naturally warm places — sunny window sills, for example — will cause flowers to spoil quickly. You should also avoid placing flowers near working fireplaces and radiators. Very draughty locations such as hearths and doorways can also cause problems.

If you need to take flowers on a journey, pack them in a box and add a synthetic ice pack to keep them cool and fresh. The flowers should not touch the ice pack.

USING OASIS

Oasis or florist's foam consists of a green porous material, which is available in pyramid, square and cylindrical shapes as well as the standard blocks 12 × 6 × 4 in (30 × 15 × 10 cm). Although some people maintain that oasis promotes an artificial, contrived look, it can be used to create natural-looking arrangements and is extremely useful for deep or awkwardly shaped containers. Oasis may also be the only means of creating certain shapes, such as those where flowers spill down over the edge of the container.

In some ways, oasis is a more "natural" medium for flowers than water. Oasis supports the stem in the same manner as earth or a branch. It holds a certain amount of water and presents it to the plant in the same way as earth: the flower draws as much water as it needs. Despite these advantages, flowers generally do not last as long in oasis as they do in water.

The size and shape of the oasis will depend on the arrangement, container, and the quantity and size of stems. For a display where you want the flowers to flow down over the edge of the container, the block or blocks of oasis must stand far enough above the top of the container that stems can be inserted at an upward angle. Oasis is easy to cut; odd shapes can be built up by covering blocks with chicken wire. Chicken wire wrapped around oasis will also prevent it from crumbling excessively; this is especially advisable for large arrangements where many stems are being inserted.

Right: A fall variation on the topiary tree combines flowers, fruit, vegetables and foliage. The "trunk" is a log set in quick-drying cement in an ordinary flowerpot.

Above: An elegant townhouse wreath composed of dried magnolia leaves matches the gun-metal paint of the door.

After the oasis has been cut to size, it should be thoroughly soaked. Float the block on top of a sink or bucket of water. The oasis will become saturated in a matter of minutes. Do not push the oasis down to submerge it as this will cause air blocks.

Before you begin an arrangement, think about which direction you want the flowers to fall. Mentally divide the oasis in sections and insert the flowers in the relevant portion. Avoid crossing stems. A haphazard approach will create problems: the display will lack stability and the oasis will be more likely to break up.

Insert each stem by holding it low down and feeding it into the oasis. Do not try to insert the flower by pushing down from the head – the stem may buckle or even break. You need to insert at least 1½ or 2 inches (4-5 cm) of stem into the oasis so that the flower has a good chance of absorbing water. To insert thick stems you may have to make a hole first with a pointed tool.

The oasis should sit in a container filled with water. Top up the level daily, pouring water over the oasis as well as into the container. If the oasis is allowed to dry out, it is difficult to restore the necessary capillary action. Flower heads can be sprayed with a plant spray. Oasis cannot be reused, but it is cheap and widely available.

CHICKEN WIRE

Chicken wire is standard florist's equipment and has many varied uses. If a large arrangement needs to be transported, chicken wire wrapped around the oasis will prevent it from crumbling. Chicken wire also makes a good alternative to oasis for creating large displays. The wire should be crumpled and tangled so that the flowers remain stable.

Chicken wire also allows you to use a few flowers, or flowers with fine stems, in a wide-necked container. If the container is opaque, a ball of chicken wire pushed down inside will hold the flowers in place. For a glass container, you can lay a mesh of chicken wire over the neck and arrange the flowers within the grid. The wire can be disguised with moss. (Alternatively, you can construct the grid with plastic tape.)

WATER VIALS

Water vials, test tubes or "thimbles" are small glass containers of the type which are often seen enclosing the stems of orchids. They are available in about four sizes to suit different stems. The special advantage of vials is that they allow cut flowers to be combined with potted displays. The vial is inserted in the earth or basket to hold water for the cut flowers. The vial must be in an upright position and topped up daily with water. For a large arrangement, a small jam jar makes a good alternative.

WIRING

Wiring flowers consists of removing the stems and attaching lightweight wire to the flower head. The technique is mostly used for making wedding bouquets and headdresses, and for dried flower arrangements. Time-consuming, intricate, and demanding quite different skills from those used in flower arranging, wiring is best left to the professionals, especially for weddings.

Many people believe that wiring inevitably results in a stiff, unnatural-looking bouquet, but such rigid constructions are merely poor examples of the technique. It is perfectly possible to wire flowers so that they retain a sense of movement and fluidity. The great advantage of wiring is that it is possible to create trailing or curving shapes. And because the stems are removed, bouquets are considerably lighter and more comfortable to carry and headdresses are easier to wear for long periods. Wiring also helps avoid the flowers from becoming battered and gives extra support when they begin to wilt.

The wire must be strong enough to support the flower, but not rigid. There are over twenty gauges of wire, from fine silver for wiring tiny agapanthus florets to heavier steel for attaching large carnation heads. In a bouquet, individual wires are drawn together and taped to make a comfortable handle. Special florist's tape is used which bonds together in warmth of the hand.

The florist will be able to advise as to which flowers are suitable for wired bouquets or headdresses. The loss of stem shortens the life of flowers and certain species such as scabious will not survive once the stems are removed.

Below: Twisted vines bound with brocade are decorated with preserved magnolia leaves, cones, roses, dried celosia, cinnamon sticks and terracotta bells in an exercise in textural combination.

Index

Numbers in italics refer to photographs

achillea (Yarrow; *Achillea* sp.),
12, 31, 50, *51*
alchemilla mollis, 31, *32*, 33
alstroemeria (Peruvian lily;
Alstroemeria hybrid), 12, 21,
57, *103*
amaranthus (*Amaranthus* sp.),
12, 31; dried, 52, *53*
amaryllis (*Hippeastrum* hybrids),
12, *55*, 57, *103*, *105*
anemone (*Anemone coronaria*),
12, 29, 31, *54*, 57, 72, *73*
anthurium, 77
antirrhinums, *63*
apple, 6, 60, 80, *81*, 84, *85*, 90,
91, 92, *93*; wreath 77, 80, *81*
Apple Harvest, 92, *93*
Apple Wreath, 80, *81*
artichokes, 31
Asparagus Basket, 96, *97*
asparagus 96, *97*; fern 44, 62
aster (Michaelmas daisy; *Aster
novia-belgii*), 12, 77
astilbe, *61*, 64, *65*
aubergine, 29, 68, *69*
Australian Arrangement, 34, *35*
azalea 50, *51*, *55*, 78, 96, *97*

banksia, 12
basic techniques 100-111
beans, 29
beech, 31, 33, *59*, 60
begonia rex, *28*, 44, *45*, 62
berries, 6, 8, 25, *28*, 29, 58, 60,
63, 77, 78, 84, *85*, 86, *87*
blackberries, *25*, 29, *61*
botrytis, 10
box (*Buxus sempervirens*), 13, 21
brodiaea, 13

cabbage (*lollo rosso*), 29, 58, 62
camellia 92, *93*
Candlelight, 66, *67*
carnation (*Dianthus* sp.), 14, 21,
57, 62; 'clove', 44, *45*
celosia (*Celosia argentea*

hybrids), 14, *25*, 31, 68, *69*,
103, *109*
chestnuts, 6, 10, *25*, 29, 33, 58
chickenwire, 52, 70, 94, 98, 108
chrysanthemum
(*Chrysanthemum* hybrids), 10,
11, 14, 21, *23*, *25*, 29, 57, 62,
63, 77, 78, 79, 90, *91*, *102*, *105*
cinnamon sticks, *109*
Classical Urn, 98, *99*
colour, *24*
cones, 94, *95*, *109*
containers, 26
Contemporary Design, 42, *43*
corndolly, 77
cornflower, 31
crab apple (*Malus* sp.), 14
cranberries, 68, *69*
creeper, 70, *71*
cupressus, 21, 62
cutting and conditioning, 102
cyclamen, 36, *37*, 62
cynara (*Cynara scolymus*), 14, 31

daises, *25*, 62
dahlia (*Dahlia* hybrids), *15*, 86,
87
delphinium (*Delphinium elatum*
hybrids), 31
dogwood (*Cornus alba*), 42, *43*,
74
"double leg mount", 33
dried flowers, 6, 8, 22, 29, 31, 54,
62, 78; foliage and leaves, 52,
53; flowers suitable for home
drying, 31; working with, 33;
drying methods, 32, 33, 56
Dried Garland, 52, *53*
Dried Roses, 46, *47*
driftwood, *28*, 86, *87*

echinops (Globe-thistle;
Echinops ritro), *15*, 31
elaeagnus (*Elaeagnus* sp.), *15*, 57
eryngium (*Eryngium* sp.), 16, 48,
49

eucalyptus, 9, 21, *24*, 34, *35*, 62
euphorbia (*Spurgens Euphorbia
fulgens*), 16, *24*, 57, 78, *79*, 103

Fall Cascade, 70, *71*
Fall Palette, the, 12-21
fern, *100*
figs, 68, *69*
florist 8, 10, 25, 28, 56, 78; wire,
29
freesia (*Freesia* hybrids), 16, 21,
33, 57
freeze drying, 31
fruit, 6, 22, *25*, *28*, 29, 40, *41*, 58,
60, 77, 78, 86, 94, *95*, *107*
Fruit Baskets, 40, *41*

Game Table, 86, *87*
gardenia, 33
gerbera (Transvaal daisy;
Gerbera jamesonii), 16, *25*
gifts, 78
gladiolus (Sword lily; *Gladiolus*
hybrids), 16, 21, 26, 57
glycerining (*see* dried flowers –
drying methods)
gourds, 6, 29, 40, *41*, 77
grapes, 96, *97*
grasses, *28*, 40, *41*, 60, 77
greenhouse, 32
gypsophila (baby's breath;
Gypsophila), 21, 31, 33, 58
Guy Fawkes night, 74, 77, 80

Hanging Decoration, 68, *69*
Hallowe'en party, 77, 80, 84
harvest festival, 22, *25*, 68, *74*,
100
heather (*Erica* sp.), 16, *22*, 31, 48,
49, 57, *63*, 64, *65*, 72, *73*, 94,
95; dried, 52, *53*
hebe (*Hebe* sp.), 17, 57
helichrysum (Straw flower;
Helichrysum bracteatum), 17,
31; dried 32, 52, *53*, *59*
honesty, 31

honeysuckle (*Lonicera* spp.), 11,
50, *51*, 58, 82, *83*
hops, *56*, 60, 70, *71*
hothouse blooms, 10, 60
hydrangea (*Hydrangea* sp.), 17,
31, *32*, 33, 48, *49*, *61*, 64, *65*,
88, *89*

Impromptu Table Setting, 88, *89*
Indian Summer, 50, *51*
iris, 21
ivy (*Hedera helix*)
"Arborescens"), 9, 11, 18, 21,
25, 34, *35*, 42, *43*, *54*, *55*, 57,
60, 66, *67*, 70, *71*, 72, *73*, 78,
86, *87*, 88, *89*, 92, *93*, 96, *97*,
103

jasmine 50, *51*, 82, *83*

"kangaroo paws", 34, *35*
kiln drying, 31
larkspur, 31
lavender (*Lavandula
angustifolia*), 18, *30*, 31
laurel, 21
leeks, 29
lichen, 42, *43*, *74*, 98, *99*
lily (Asiatic lily; *Lilium* sp.), 18, 21,
57, 77; arum, *24*;
"Casablanca", *24*, 36, *37*;
"Rosita", *25*
love-lies-bleeding (*Amaranthus
caudatus* hybrids), 18, 57, *60*;
dried, 68, *69*

magnolia, 31, 33, *108*, *109*
maple (*Acer* sp.), 8, 18, 60
marigolds, 50, *51*, 72, *73*
moss, 21, 29, 33, 42, *43*, *74*, 76,
78, 80, *81*, 82, *83*, 84, *85*, 86,
87, 90, *91*, 94, *95*, 108; bun, 38,
39, 66, *67*, 98, *99*; sphagnum,
52, *53*

New Look, 44, *45*
nigella (love-in-a-mist; *Nigella*

damascena), 31, *59*
nuts, 28, 29, 33, 60, *76, 77*

oak (*Quercus* sp.) 18, 60, 64, *65*, 90, *91*
oasis (or florist's foam), 29, 33, 38, 50, 66, 68, 70, 82, 86, 92, 96, 98, 106, 108
onions, 98, *99*
orchid, 21
Outdoor Party, 90, *91*

pansies, 66, *67*
party flowers, 77
peony, 31, *59*
pheasant's feathers, 78, 86, *87*
phlox, 50, *51*
pine cones, 6, 28, 98, *99*
plant spray, 50
plums, 96, *97*
pomegranates, 25, 96, *97*, 98, *99*
poppy (*Papaver* sp.), 18, 31
privet (*Ligustrum* sp.), 19
protea (*Protea* sp.), 19, *27*, 31, 38, *39*

pumpkins, 29

ranunculus (*Ranunculus asiaticus* hybrids), 20, 31, 57, 92, *93*
redcurrants, 68, *69*
red cauliflower, 96, *97*
red potatoes, 96, *97*
rhododendron, *9*
rose (*Rosa* sp.), 20, 21, 28, 31, 32, 56, 57, 58, 62, 70, *71, 74,* 78, *79,* 82, *83,* 96, *97,* 98, *99,* 102, *109;* 'Blue Moon', 64, *65;* dried, *30,* 46, *47, 59, 76;* miniature, 50, *51, 60,* 66, *67,* 68, *69, 78*
rosehips, 6, *11,* 44, *45, 54, 55,* 60, 78, *79,* 86, *87,* 90, *91, 103*
Rose Tree, 82, *83*
rushes, 40, *41*

scabious, 48, *49,* 109
sedum, 78, *79,* 82, *83*
selecting flowers, 8, 10
Shades of Blue, 48, *49*
silica gel, 33, 56
Silvery Display, 36, *37*

skimmia (*Skimmia japonica*), 21, *28,* 55, 57, 96, *97,* 98, *99*
Special Occasions, 74-99
statice (Everlasting; *Limonium sinuatum*), 21, 29, 31; "sea lavender", 21
swedes, 98, *99*

Table Garland, 94, *95*
table settings, 78
temperature, 106
terracotta pots, 26, 77, 84
Thanksgiving, 74, 78, 80
Three in a Row, 38, *39*
Tied Bouquet, 64, *65*
trailing foliage, 88, *89*
types of arrangement, 26-29

vegetables, 6, 22, 25, 28, 29, 40, 58, 60, 77, *107*
viburnum (*Viburnum tinus*), 21, 57, 64, *65,* 102
vines, 11, *109*
violets, 66, *67*
virginia creeper (*Parthenocissus*

quinquefolia), 21, 28, *54, 55,* 57, 58

year round flowers, 21

water, 104
water vials, 109
weddings, fall, 54-73; bouquets and headdresses, 33, 56, 58, 59, 60, 64, *65,* 109; flowers, 56; suitable flowers and foliage, 57; bride's flowers, 58-9; attendants' flowers, 60; flowers for the ceremony, 60, 62; flowers for the reception, 62, 63
wheat (*Triticum* sp.), 21, *22,* 31; garlands, 58; stems, 77, *77,* 80, *81*
wheatsheaves, 25, 29, 60, 77, *77*
Wicker Wreath, 84, *85*
willow, 29
wiring, 29, 33, 109
wood varnish, 33
woody stems, 102
wreaths, *76,* 78; wicker, 84

Acknowledgements

With special thanks to Liz Wilhide, Di Lewis, Kirsty Craven, Hilary Guy, Paul Morgan and the wonderful team at Pavilion Books, who have made working on this book such fun.

To all who have allowed me to ransack their homes for 'the sake of art', and to everyone slaving away at 56 James Street; Lucinda, Tracey, Andrea, Mark, Sam and Claire, without whom this book would have been impossible.

To my parents, Maurice and Brenda, and my sister Jill for their never-ending support.

Finally, to Linda Smith for the 'palette' illustrations, and to Gill Elsbury for the line illustrations.

Jane Packer

The Publishers gratefully acknowledge the following for providing locations for photography:

Mr and Mrs Charles Fry, Chaddington, Wiltshire
Miss Chapman, East Farley Church, East Farley, Nr Maidstone, Kent
Jon and June Summerill, London
Karen and Derek MacDonald, Corpusty, Norfolk
Jane and Howard Heathfield, Corpusty, Norfolk
Charlotte and Henry Crawley, Hunworth, Norfolk
Jackie and David Attfield, Thornage, Norfolk.
Photograph on page 7 is by kind permission
of the Sunday Express Magazine.